Cold Storage

COLD STORAGE

POEMS BY

KEITH ALTHAUS

Off the Grid Press

Boston, Massachusetts

Off the Grid Press is an imprint of Grid Books.

Grid Books
86 Glendower Road
Boston, MA 02131

www.grid-books.org

Many of the poems in this book have been previously published as follows:

Magazines:
    Drunken Boat: The Age of Acronyms; In a Little While
    Harvard Review: Preparing the Body
    Hotel Amerika: The Boxes; Speakers, Banners
    Meridian: If I Could Throw My Voice
    Orion: Rain; The Etymology of Halo
    Phantom Limb: 23 Wall Street
    Plume: Artificial Light; Holy Day; A Strange Place
    Ploughshares: Elegy for No One; New Year's Underground; On a Photograph of Gurdjieff in a Bookstore
        Window; This Candle; To One Who Owes Me Money; Fragment
    Provincetown Arts: From the Pilgrim Monument
    Zoland: Elbows
Anthologies:
    Aspects of Robinson: Fall of the Magician
    Pushcart 33: Rain

Front cover painting: Susan Baker, *From Cold Storage* (detail), oil on canvas, 2001, collection of the artist.

Printed by Cushing-Malloy, Inc., Ann Arbor, Michigan. Book design by Michael Alpert.

ISBN: 978-0-9778429-9-5

TABLE OF CONTENTS

I

II

III

for Ellery

I

THE ETYMOLOGY OF HALO

What you are working towards,
even in those hours spent
staring into the void
hoping to bring back strength
to hold down impulse
and raise the spirit
through a rain of blows,
comes not from heaven,
nor is that ring from
the finger of god, but is
instead a circle worn
on the threshing floor,
a path poor animals
made by constant turning.

A STRANGE PLACE

Sometimes you feel
a drop out of nowhere
on your skin
even on a clear day,
but because
it is just one
and gone instantly,
you don't think about it,
it doesn't stay
like déjà vu, that room
imposed on yours,
so when you enter one
you enter both.

Watchmen
who've fallen asleep
so often, so deep,
sometimes wake
not knowing where
or who they are.
That moment
a drop could fall.

Earth becomes more beautiful
as it gets older,
age doesn't matter to it,
it's already absurdly ancient,
but instead of appearing
stale and tired,
it feels fresh, new,

like the same words
shifting back and forth
between question
and answer.

And I can't tell you
if you ask,
whether this
child's collection—
pinecones, feathers, shells—
is about life or death.

AFTER RILKE

The room is lit only
when the door opens
to let someone out,
and then
just for a moment
before it's pitch again.

In that instant
we see ourselves
briefly, limbs before us
examining what
we've only felt
in the dark, a thought
making its way
into words.

NEW YEAR'S UNDERGROUND

This subway map
reminds me
of the colored stripes
on hospital floors
that guide us
to recovery
or dead ends
(I lift my glass
to the amber line)
or the spacious room
that overlooks
a beautiful parking lot
where the car roofs
are like tiles
you'll soon be walking on
in the same sunshine,
just a little older,
paler, having seen
the blizzard of empty beds,
too much aluminum,
so many shaky starts.

In this howling tunnel
they come into focus:
lemon, pink, lime,
the corner where a couple
stands aside to let you pass,
motioning you forward
while murmuring *red,*
red, waiting for
their strength to return.

The lines are like the nerves
and veins themselves
that are having trouble now,
that somehow got intertwined
or clogged, yet here they
cross without difficulty
or getting tangled up or lost,
regrouping at the intersection,
then heading off again
on separate missions,
sometimes shadowing
each other for awhile
until the lungs pull away
from the heart
with a jolt like a train.

Underground,
below the city streets,
stores, and high-rises,
the celebration leads
to sober reflection,
reassessments and the desire
to work to change,
but not today, where
we're sandwiched between
the past and what's not
yet arrived.
I'm lost
between the revelers
with one more stop,
and those who've
already had their cup
of sweetness on a tray.

PREPARING THE BODY

I'm feeding it,
making sure
the hair is combed,
keeping it warm,
clothed, and clean,
till it's ready
to give up
this running about,
constant getting
in and out of cars,
answering the phone,
the endless back and forth,
to finally lie
behind a door
that is always closed,
like *trompe l'oeil*
painted on the sides
of houses
just south of Genoa,
where we were lost
and annoyed
at being fooled
by two worlds.

IF I COULD THROW MY VOICE

like a ventriloquist,
I would make it speak
through the lamp

beside your bed,
when moonlight
chisels features

on the marble pillow
with its chiaroscuro
deepening the edges,

leaving high cheekbones
and flat planes
sunken and breathing solemnly

while the heart
roars like a furnace
fed the memories of a lifetime.

And I would have it say
I am sorry for the place you're in,
the strings that pull you

out of bed each morning,
wake you in someone else's arms,
and I would tell you that it's me

who hovers near
when in between
the carefully designated minutes

of your day a blank appears
like the unfinished pre-dawn sky
that hasn't decided

if it's white or gray or blue,
and for a few moments
cradling your coffee you

think of nothing, miss nothing,
look forward to nothing,
and I would

cut the strings right there
and let you stay,
attended by a ghost

that envelops
and protects you like
the fog off the bay

which softens and erases
edges, corners, faces,
which don't register, words

that don't belong,
including these from
who knows where.

IN A LITTLE WHILE

In a little while
the light will go out behind these faces
I've talked with all afternoon,
including mine,
and the well
we draw our voices from
will run dry.

The luster
you look for
in the eye of the porgy
and sea bass
on a bed of ice
will cloud
with new incomprehension,
and the chaos of a sunbeam
strained through a lens
will cut this leaf in half
like a hand of fire.

TOURIST POEM

All truths are half-truths,
part of each lies in the shadow of the teller.
Heisenberg told us that.
You saw half of the Sistine Chapel,
or the Doges' Palace, the other half
was hidden behind a scaffold
or wrapped in a giant tarp.
Years later the missing part
was displayed, restored, grand,
almost gaudy, and the half you'd seen
disappeared behind a screen.

From the parking lot
at Cold Storage Beach in Truro
you can see the sun going down
and the moon rising, and in between
the puny beams of Highland Light
like a persistent, solitary firefly.

Our eyes can't see what's going on
behind them unless they're turned
inward as in sleep, toward dreams,
whose furniture and settings
change with each day's jostling
in the street, like the twisting
of a kaleidoscope, whose bits we know
though not their combinations.

RAIN

Rain is the great transporter,
even before it arrives
its perfume slips under the door
like a letter, an invitation to rise
as earthbound drops
descend like weights
backstage, raising the scenery
and lifting us out of easy chairs
and easy lives
to where it never rains,
is always parched, a room
cut off and boarded up,
and where a single drop
on those lips
could bring you back.

DIVINATION

Coins tossed
in lieu of yarrow stalks
rolled under the rug
and behind the tub
in the kitchen;
worth less today
than when they
wobbled off
in search of fortunes.

Ripping up linoleum,
tearing out the plumbing,
you may uncover one
of these harbingers,
now tarnished from lack
of human contact.

It is always the future
in that room for rent
with its stack of cheap
holy books toppled over
into steps, shoplifted
or overdue, wisdom
unaltered, undiluted
by the blood of martyrs
or the spray of the whirlpool
of words spun from
the translator's ear.

There should be a great map somewhere,
a whole electric wall, blinking

all the time, of just these places,
sacred to a few, unknown to most,
a diagram that connects the dots
like a constellation of burned-out bulbs
that once spelled paradise,
this one included, though
not set apart, but buried in the city,
so even after its demise
it's still occupied, the way animals
move into each other's nests.

A scent survives
along with ash on tables
spattered with wax.
The walls are free of the shadows
which used to climb
in imitation of a stalk
of incense swaying
in the draft
of young breath,
sliding sideways,
sweeping the room
like a vine
reaching for
something in the air.

II

FATE

Without tearing a limb,
or losing a button,
you dropped me
in the middle of Astor Place
and never said why.

It's a question for the freak
whose head is half-melted
and doesn't care for questions
anymore, who's found
a new way of answering:
pressing himself against
whatever's near: pavement,
dirt, stone wall, gates
of hell, all hard enough
to feel the texture, taste
the smell, have it leave
its imprint on the skin,
the intaglio of what's real.

The door ahead
like a letter edged in black
but transposed and standing upright
surrounded by light.
Does that mean only good things
lie in store
for whoever opens it?
Or just that appearances
are for the birds?
We make our own light,

as much as we can stand,
and fate is what
would have happened anyway.

A HANDFUL OF GRAVEL

The day's magic:
fairy dust
or just
the pink
eraser crumbs
that make a name,
an address,
vanish.

The block
you stumbled on:
windows & doors
reflecting
back and forth
across the traffic,
infinity's
fake façade.

Run your fingers along
the goose-bumped flesh
of stairwell walls,
the hard sea-green enamel,
trailing dirt and grime
from stoop
to rooftop clothesline:
skirts and sheets
pollinated with soot.

When you arrive
at the last memory

will it be shiny,
bright, having been
hidden all this time,
or dark, confused,
as a tarnished mirror
no one's looked into
for years?

A handful of gravel mid-air,
tossed at the darkened window,
a constellation
real as those
that control our destiny.

In a year
this will be woven
into the fabric
of what's over.
And their failure,
falling back,
like the beginning
of an avalanche,
is the failure of all
returning to a path.

ON A PHOTOGRAPH OF GURDJIEFF
IN A BOOKSTORE WINDOW

The dome, the mustache
like a circus strongman's,
those shoulders people still climb on,
and eyes that hold you
in the snow before stacked
and battered volumes of mutually
exclusive systems of belief:
UFOs, black magic, Madame
Blavatsky's wisdom received
at the feet of lamas, while
yours grow cold in the slushy street.
His look follows passersby
who, though they can't identify
the man or recognize
the eyes which leapt
to music, movement, dance,
still stop in the sidewalk,
as if on command.

ILLUMINATION

In the zendo
they seek illumination
by sitting,
emptying themselves,
readying the vessel.
In Italy
you can buy it
for a few coins.
Almost every church
has some painted panel,
or whole wall
that comes alive, sparkles
when money drops
into the metal box
clanking like a city bus
and a bank of lights
comes on.
Neither
lasts long enough,
one only exists
outside of Time,
the other is wholly time,
always running out.
Yet to both
crowds clamber
from afar, or from
just across the nave,
to see something
obscure made plain,
at least temporarily.

So when the lights shut off
we turn to leave amazed
and squeeze our eyes
to see on the nearest dark,
it lingering, then fade.

ARTIFICIAL LIGHT

filled those rooms
yet we couldn't see
where the shadows went.
If the real is unreal,
or at least temporal,
nature must be false,
and only the ideal,
which is nowhere, exists.
So the thinking goes,
in circles, quicker than
a mouse whose whole
existence is a blur
or dead stop on a doorstep
after a life of running,
suddenly too slow
to pull a needle out
of a haystack,
or an arm stuck
in salute like the scarecrow
pointing both ways
without conviction.

A.I.R.

A.I.R. = artist-in-residence:
a New York Fire Department designation
placed above the entrances
of commercial buildings to indicate
the presence of legal living lofts.

1.

The coveted plaques
over doors
recessed
in the canyons
of the city
stand out
like signs of life
after hours,
or signals
between members
of a secret society,
like pisces
scratched on Roman walls,
or the crayon scrawl
on the torn box flap
stuck in a window
on the Bowery
proclaiming
"Eye-openers are back."

2.

You never traveled
to the lower level
of Weiser's Bookshop,
or held that
in a certain valley
in the Hindu Kush,
behind a waterfall
there is a door
that leads
to the powerhouses
of the East
where Initiates
toil ceaselessly
to keep the world aloft,
their prayer wheels
and chanting
fuels souls
unaware they ever
were in peril.

3.

But you subscribe
because of this
elementary abbreviation
to the belief
that somewhere inside,
behind the brick
or cast iron façade,
someone thinks as you,

though not exactly:
but in line and color,
in spatial relationships,
if not the specific
blue and yellow
that stains your fingers
this morning,
or the shapes and forms
you wrestled with last night,
until the colorless dawn
from which city days are made,
their sun the aggregate
of the leftover glow
of streetlamps and headlights
mixed with the glue
of the ground up glints
and sparkle of broken glass,
while the curve
of a jagged bottle
echoes the arc
of space upon which
the mind can wreck
or save itself.

4.

After all these years
the air unchanged,
still lighter on Mondays,
now with the gloss
of a fair departing,
the glow of voices

carried along a string
tied to the belly buttons
of balloons that burst,
their captions
strewn in the gutter
with fliers for events
that happened only once,
but whose coming
is endlessly announced.

5.

Like the to and fro
of brushstrokes
the crosshatching of the street,
the slow building of a surface,
the application of impasto,
the backing up in snow
of trucks, all sizes, colors,
to the loading dock,
accompanied by beeping now,
but still following a guy
gesturing in mirrors,
all day long until
like a spell lifted
the vibrations cease
at five o'clock,
metal doors spring open
and a horde (the opposite
of miners, slow to enter)
races for the entrance
to the underground,

seeking the gold
of private life.

6.

You will never see
figures quite
like us again
trudging up
the street
with laundry
bags and duffle
bags, scavenging
firewood for our stoves,
among the curbside
heaps of broken pallets,
yet that trail survives,
fossilized
in layers
of immortal snow.

ELBOWS

What's become of the men
who used their elbows
to push through the crowd
to the bar at *Stanley's*,
or prop up heavy heads
above the lacquered tables
of the *Annex*,
supporting brains tired
from a day storming the page,
now full of small talk
about big things
& vice versa—
the prematurely hip
with wire rims and army jackets,
and discouraged partners
whose book-lined dreams
aged gracelessly in the shadows
of unfinished theses,
novels whose constant tunneling
has finally grown airless.
Quick and sharp,
angled for making room
or driving home a point,
where are those elbows now,
collapsed into powder
in the corners of a suit
lying flat in the city of the dead
surrounding the city of the living
in which there is no *Stanley's*
or *Annex* anymore?

TO ONE WHO OWES ME MONEY

To finally locate you
after all these years
and then—
it's in a dream!—
you're near the end
in a hospital
in a small New England city,
what monstrous snake
of a road led you here,
where you sit on the bed
making calls as you did,
to the rich and famous,
trying to raise money
for your wife's pathetic project,
and by extension, us, laboring
within earshot of your makeshift
desk. They were never home
to you, always at lunch
or in a meeting. I don't think
I ever heard you get through
to anyone. It was forty years ago.
The money you owe me would
be a fortune now. I could use it.
But I needed it then, as I have
almost every year since.
You used it to run away
with your wife and daughter
to England, and then
with your daughter
away from your wife

back to America.
You were a fool under her spell,
and when the spell was broken…
well, we all fear the day
the endearing, idiosyncratic traits
turn to irritants and hideous faults,
the way a clown's face goes
to scary after funny. We loaned
you strength on those filthy floors
overlooking Second Avenue,
tearing down walls, pulling
through the lathing old horse hair
from the century before,
as outside it went from winter
to spring and early summer,
and all we took away were
a few indelible songs
from the radio, news
that kept getting shriller,
and a sense that what happened here
would always be tested, weighed
against another life that spoke
in anger and in silence,
and whose outstretched claw
you passed each day in the street.
Painting, sheet-rocking, we gave
up months of life's best season: youth.
Now you've returned the only way
you could to pay your debt, and left
this poem. We'll call it even.

III

DISAPPEARING SOON

not as the lunch counters,
or ashtrays full of sand
or melting snow
which regroups at night
into smaller, sharper particles
until there are just a few
rhinestones scattered on the lawn,
but as a face,
brushed away before
we can forget it.

Walking among us
are people who have
been to the moon.
They look like you and me.
Eyes which have seen
the lumpy lunar surface
are as dull and unknowing
as our own.

They too hear
what's left of bells,
their coarser, outer rings
wobbling off-center
where music melds with everything:
backfires, squealing tires,
voices on the corner raised
to overcome the street, the joy
that coincides with noise.

HOLY DAY

A holy day
not on any calendar
but in the middle
of January's
deep freeze
when the woods
resound with cracks
like rifle fire
and their ricochet;
a sudden thaw
and the air's
an inert element
picking up the scent
and traces
of the earth again
carrying them
beyond the bower
of broken limbs
and branches
to where heavy green
is remembered,
resurrected for a day,
an hour, under the sky
watermarked with floaters,
and illumined
by a worn sun
and tarnished moon,
the worthless coinage
of the old regime

whose loyal followers
hold their once-a-year
parade today.

RELICS

Scattered among hill towns
in somber sunlight, guarded
by thick walls and congealed
shadows in cities, here a bone,
there a lock of hair, a fingernail,
piece of skin, molten
when flayed, now dry and cold
in an elaborate gilt cage.

If gathered all together
would they make one whole saint
who could be brought back—
though why and what for?
Only to be martyred
in some newfangled way,
and dispersed again, the gruesome
wealth redistributed to other towns
where people would line up
to see a new ending to an ancient story.

The itinerant painters of the Renaissance
trudged from town to town,
up and down hills like these, leaving
if you can believe, a trail of light,
though the story out of sequence.
One palette for saints and sinners,
the same yellow for the tips of flames
and the halo's blinding rim.

FROM THE PILGRIM MONUMENT

for Roger Skillings

The climb is breathtaking,
the view roughly medieval:
on one side, the town's
boat-filled harbor
and traffic-clogged streets;
on the other, graveyards,
mute and still, stretching to the edge
of the moon-like dunes,
forever changing, shifting,
being taken away (the tallest one
already halved since we arrived here
thirty years ago) and nothing
added or put back except
beach grass planted to slow
the process, and a little dust,
ashes of friends who loved it here,
and wanted to stay or go
wherever it is going.

YUCCA

sign high,
in the traffic island
outside of Provincetown:
guides, like martyrs, born to fail.
The tons of air
bouncing off semi walls
hardly sway the stalks,
let alone the plastic flowers
around the marker
of someone young,
small, or slow.

What nourishes these
machine-pressed petals,
rosettes, and molded ferns,
that in turn
echo the wreaths of human hair
on display
in the museum below
the Monument
where they creep
the schoolchildren out,
used to blood and gore
but unprepared for these
Victorian expressions of grief.

The yucca,
like the Monument itself,
ostentatious, out of all proportion
to the landscape,

ridiculous, towering, priapic;
their blossoms falling
like paper lanterns
in a garden
shaken loose by a gust
and driven out
like fleeing guests.

FRAGMENT

You could be rowing across a parking lot
full of strangers who don't see you,
or drifting silently through the thick walls
of an institution, when you reach that shore.

And whatever you have on, even
a plain hospital gown, that will be your robe
for the ceremony that takes place in your
last breath, held before you like a lantern.

FALL OF THE MAGICIAN

Water is slate, far down.
—Weldon Kees

One great trick—
you can make your life disappear.
There's no one to thank for this.
No one thinks of it
except you, or if
they're suddenly removed
from their element
and going uphill slowly
around traffic cones
(they're working
on the Sagamore Bridge again),
and the water down there,
kept from us, is still
as the roof of another world.

ELEGY FOR NO ONE

So many have died,
to pick out one
seems willful,
unkind, and besides
you might forget
the friend you promised
never to forget,
so let this be
for anyone who died
in this season of death,
which from now on
will be full of faces
coming forward,
smiling from the page
like the line hastily
formed backstage
that stands before
the curtain and bows,
then follows its spot
back into the shade
of scenery and props.

REMINDER

They put a clock
beside you
in your bed,
a reminder
of your mother's
heartbeat. The loud
ticking was supposed
to help you sleep
not keep you awake,
but how could that
cold metal sound like
her soft breath
or whisper? Now
it's the back-beat
that follows you
into the street
where it drowns
arguing horns,
the noise of crowds,
but not the steps
on sidewalks
late at night
that prove the world
is hollow.

THIS CANDLE

In the end
there is always
a little change
left in the pockets,
a few suns and moons
you couldn't spend.

Nearby
the cloud
of a would-be breath
doesn't move,
reprieved
but useless.

This candle
will change all that,
use the last bit
of air for light,
and heat the hand
that shields the eyes
and face when it gets
too close or bright.

No one speak.
The dark
will say a few words
about our friend,
leave it at that.

IV

SPEAKERS, BANNERS

America with a K.
The hillside moving.

Grass of battlefield and playground,
wet in the morning, dry by afternoon.

The life cycle of a leaflet:
machine delivered,
dispersed by hand,
torn, scattered by sunset.
A moth's is longer.

Return if you can,
like the lifetime of keys weighing down a drowning man,
to whom they belong,
those years.

THE AGE OF ACRONYMS

Alphabet blocks tumble
from a child's hand like dice,
bounce and settle in the carpet,
coming up a once familiar
combination, call letters
of the left, now unnoticed
even by the grownups at the table
who go on commenting
on her hair, her eyes, the pretty
pajamas, while the letters rage
outside their universe.

One by one,
she turns them over
like rival factions
splintered from
those now face down,
which failed
because the world
wasn't ready, hadn't hit
the critical mass of misery
and avoidable suffering,
so *they* died, expiring
in halls with too many chairs,
placards, leaflets,
fire consuming
thought then words.

Blocks with letters raised,
so you can read them

in the dark,
feel between the rims
the wavy wooden grain
bleeding through the paint,
and in that sea
imagine faces, friends
from the end of being true,
marching together under a sign.

Cloudy afternoon,
wind-swept streets
clear of cars and people,
lonely as after a war, the victory
rats and cockroaches share.

It all comes back:
the banner dropped,
one side let go,
the run to shelter,
there is none,
all you know,
there is more,
this is just a bubble,
an unlikely spot
on earth whose other places
fester, glisten
like initials slick with rain
inside a heart.

23 WALL STREET

The missing chunks of granite
do not exist, except
a Whiteread undertakes
to cast them now
in the deadly pallor
of Plaster of Paris,
or unless a few
were saved, to view
in horror, or to honor
the memory lost
a little every day as
we go by without notice
where the anarchist
drew his cart next to
the walls of Morgan Bank
and blew it up, horse
and all, in service of
an ideal which may already
have come to pass
and now has passed away:
success being the rung
before oblivion.

THE BOXES

"The Communist Party USA Donates Its Archives to NYU"
—Headline, March 2007

1.

Stephen Hawking said
he once believed
when the universe ceases to expand
and starts contracting
Time would reverse itself
and run backwards,
then he reversed himself.
But for some
it has already begun.
For them there is only the past,
the present
is to pick through,
not for clues as to
what went wrong
and how to fix it,
too late for that,
or to re-ignite a faith
grown cold,
though possibly
more beautiful
now it's dead:
a corpse not to be revived,
like those "end of the world" cults
who after their humiliation
regroup and recalculate the end

with bruised enthusiasm,
but more like the pack
of young archivists,
white-gloved as mimes
who'll eagerly uncover
your mistakes, a few
successes too perhaps,
as both enemies
and friends depart.

Let them preserve:
a group photo on a farm,
in a railway station,
at a camp,
smiles,
caught in an idyll,
when almost everyone
was young, and for
a moment agreed
on almost everything.

2.

In History's care at last:
the contents of these files,
but in boxes too uniform
and pristine—
the way the rich would move,
not in cartons
from the liquor store,
but acid-free, archival cases
in which they'll cease to age,

be treated to neutralize
the acidity of old paper,
erase the foxing
on broadsides,
reversing time,
and in between
taking time to identify
the faces in photographs,
if not the owner of the strand
of hair that floated down
and lodged between two pages,
and which will never turn gray
or white, though she who typed it
surely did long ago;
and the one
for whom the speech
was written and the crowd
who heard it,
banners waving, now gone,
genes dispersed
in multiplying generations,
but their memories stored here.

3.

From the needle trades,
print shops, pushcarts,
the refuse of a hall,
butts and stubs, paper cups
like dunce caps;
out of argument heat rises
with smoke's artificial breath,

looking for escape.
In the finite universe,
inside the great number
of the ever-changing quantity
of particles of matter,
these boxes are included;
every word
is counted,
every letter,
every drop of ink,
each period
like a great weight
carried here:
some map has lost its cities,
some deep sea
has drained away.

SPRING LAMENT

Like the soundtrack from *The Battle of Algiers* out there tonight,
the peepers bring forth their spring chorus.
The old days hang in the closet like ghosts;
one day they'll go up in a cloud
of acrid smoke, synthetic fibers, plastic buttons.
It's burning season all the time now. Inside the skull
old cells pass on a string of remastered tunes
from the tar pits of black vinyl.
Tomorrow you'll retrieve one or two,
but tonight you've brought to life
a shade from the unliveable past.

V

FOR MARY OLIVER,
LEAVING PROVINCETOWN

Goodbye, Mary.
That's hard to say.
My mother's name was Mary.
It is also hard to see
part of your life
drift away, if only
symbolically.
You are the last
of the boundary stones
I found here.
Remember the others'
high-pitched rhetoric,
their drunkenness, sulking
and raving, storming out.
Plenty of scenes. Now
it is just you, going quietly
someplace where you'll no doubt
find sister and cousin birds,
louder, fatter, southern versions
of the same species you startled here
on your morning walks.

Therefore I expect
to learn soon
that you've discovered
in the new beauty
of that place,
something moving
just below the surface,

half fin, half claw,
which spoke to you
in a string of bubbles
and you answered in a voice
thin and rough as beach grass
anchoring a dune.

THE AUTHOR ADDRESSES A TREE

We should make a pact,
you and I,
no more frivolity
on my part,
no more lies,
not even in the service
of a greater truth to come.
We should know by now:
later equals never.

And from you:
just promise
not to succumb
too soon, or ever, to the stream
of harmful compounds
threatening your nature.

Be in spring
the beacon we remember,
not so much for light,
there's plenty of that
(even darkness glows)
but direction.
So if one day by chance
my words are stamped
upon your skin
neither of us
will be surprised or lost,
far as we may have come
from this moment

when we made a deal
and sealed it like kings
with a drop of sap.

ENDLESS BOOK

From there to here—
your handwriting
hasn't changed much,
at least when it's trying
to be legible, hoping
to be read again.

In that room
you were surrounded
by the same cheap paneling,
painted over,
pastel with knots,
and grooves half-filled,
like Stella's stripes,
deliberately imperfect,
proving what?
Our correspondences
follow us?
But you know that.
The track of names and faces,
melodies to words, held together
by the brain's baling wire
before it all
comes apart.

Baseboard heat,
new then,
another coincidence
in the sea of inconsistency,
now off

because it's spring,
almost always inadequate.

The differences: here,
the peepers' strident,
eerie siren. Good, it's
still cold enough to keep
the windows shut.
And there, a more substantial,
load-bearing silence,
heavy ground winds
away from water
and its lightness.
Yet sometimes
the snow's coarse crystals
form themselves in dunes,
and the roar of the interstate,
low and constant as surf,
crosses the field
and comes to the door
of the house where you began
the book you'll never finish.

POEM

Inconsolable rain
last night
on the house where I talked to gods,
and music leapt out
of appliances and furniture
and the walls gave up
standing still
and rolled like waves.

Then morning came
and they went back
to being objects
and I returned
to my body
and name:
an awkward fit.

THE UNDISCOVERED COUNTRY

So many come back now
they have their own networks
and support groups,
to compare, I suppose,
lights and messages, voices
from down long corridors,
tunnels they never reached the ends of,
stopped and made to go back.
That bittersweet return
colors everything.
Even the life stories of our friends
only go to fill balloons
which rise into specks
we will follow until
the sky lets them in.

FAREWELL

From the branch
a bird has been casting
and retrieving its net
all morning
catching nothing.

I wonder if it has
another song it doesn't
sing, the way we keep
some thoughts to ourselves.

I wonder who dwells
in the secret world
where recognition
precedes language,

the telepathy of music
often heard,
the well-traveled road,
where you know
what lies around the curve,
what song is next,

but not how
the broken barn
holds its ground,
and the fading tobacco sign
still calls to men in narrow ties
and wide lapels.

A man sits in a room and scans
the lines of a poem,
the tip of his pen touches
the top of every word.
A stone skips across
the mirrored pond.

AGAINST CLOSURE

Memory weakens the heart,
reliving all those scenes,
half-running up the hill,
flesh visible between
shoulders of the rescue workers,
and a cloud, far off, delivering rain
to a corner of the city. Now
would be the perfect time
to weigh those things,
in a pressure-free environment,
but with the scales missing,
or broken, chain lying
in the trays,
everything weighs the same—
nothing. So we can't
measure what we've done,
and the story, like a movie
seen a hundred times,
should lose its power,
yet still you look away,
let a shudder run through
worn flesh and bone.

THE ROAD AHEAD

You started following a light,
hearing a call from a place
far beyond your narrow bed.
And once in a while you saw
or heard it again in the street
hurrying along with envoys
from the other world,
"hastily-put-up men,"
who were actors in a play
you wandered into.
They knew their lines,
you had to improvise yours.
You did. For years
in ever smaller quarters,
cramped by desire,
weighed down by
the iron gall of letters.

Then you found equilibrium
in a storm, a torrent
blizzard where you could not see
the road ahead or behind,
and you moved in fear
and would have stopped
had not the storm
stopped before you. Now
whatever you meant,
whatever made you
follow in the first place
is gone. Your work is done.

Nothing's left but the plain gray
sky that goes on forever
and makes you long
to start again.

Keith Althaus is the author of two other poetry collections, *Rival Heavens* (Provincetown Arts Press, 1993) and *Ladder of Hours* (Ausable Press, 2005). He has received a Pushcart Prize as well as grants from the National Endowment for the Arts and the Massachusetts Foundation of the Arts. In 1969 he was one of the first Writing Fellows at the Fine Arts Work Center in Provincetown, Massachusetts. He lives on Cape Cod with his wife, the artist Susan Baker.